The Awakened Woman

by Casey S. Leasure

The Awakened Woman
First Printing 2014
ISBN: 9781628907032
Printed in the United States of America
Casey S. Leasure © Copyright 2012

Other Books by Casey S. Leasure
The Color of a Woman's Heart
ISBN: 978-0-615-43450-6
Oneness of Soul
ISBN: 978-0-615-57663-3

THIS BOOK IS PUBLISHED
BY
CASEY S. LEASURE

Dedicated

For those who dare to rise above the sun,
And rise above the stars to seek their reflection
between the worlds on a journey with their soul.

Ode to the Awakened

Woman delights in the nectar of her life.
Her heart is like a river flowing in harmony
With all that it touches.
Like an angel planting flowers beneath the sun,
Woman dances with each new dawn as if she was in
A garden of light and love.

Is it not in the fragrance of a rose that tells the story
Of the majestic woman and sprit she rides?
The wind and sails the sea of love.
Is it not the angels of heaven that chase
Her laughter and song?
Yet it is the wild creatures of the forest
That walk with her.
And the eagles who soar the sky around her.
For she is not a dream but a reality
Awakened in a new dawn.

Awakened is the woman who greets her day
With her heart.
Like the clouds who embrace the wind
And change formations.
Woman sees her changing life as art and
Soul, as her thoughts turn to light.
Her reflection journeys the sun that maps her path.

It is not the thunder of the sky you will hear.
But the freedom of woman as she rides
Upon the back of her dreams
And desires for her journey.
As the elements of nature are in
Harmony around her, she will feel the sun
In her face, in love with her thoughts.

Listen to the angels who sing of the woman that
Dreams of a journey into absolute love.
How beautiful it is to watch the stars dancing
In rhythm with the spirits that carry her through
An ocean of love and warmth.
Magnificent is the night, powerful is the calling
Of the Most High as the angels sing
"Hallelujah to the dreamer on her journey."
So beautiful is the woman who lies
With the spirits that carry her
Beyond time and space.

Woman will sing with the voice of her ancestors.
As her song will inter-twine the sun rays.
Like two loops dancing in the sky as one,
Her voice of love and oneness flows with the light
Of infinity, in the colors of her heart.

It is said; to see a woman as she truly is created
Is to see angels walk amongst us.
As they will dress themselves in flesh and bone
They were created in a Kingdom above the stars.
To listen to their whispers of love is to listen the
Treasures of their heart.
Her soul is the image of oneness her path is one
Of warmth and light.

Only the wind can mark
The spiritual journey of woman.
For her Spirit is always in motion
And flowing freely.

The soul of a woman is a majestic dance
That calls to her from the song in her heart.
Like the dancer compelled to create a story
Through movement and music.
Woman is compelled to express her love
Through the colors of her heart.

Woman does not stand her ground
In defense of her beliefs.
But will offer her hand in joy and love of her truth.
Her path is one of unity for all life
Through the colors of her heart
To all who would join her
In the dance of her journey.

Ride the spirit of new beginnings upon
The light that you are.
Your echoes of love and compassion
Will fill the sky and are written upon the sun.
Like the rain, you will feel your message
On all paths with the colors of your heart.

The moon sings to you, and the stars honor you.
As the Mother of Infinity embraces you with love.
For you have planted seeds of love and forgiveness,
And held your plow and hoe through
Sun and storm.
You have cultivated the crops of your life through
Laughter and hardship to which each fall you rise.
And stood in the field of your heart
Stronger each time.
Behold woman, now is your time, the universe
And all the elements will join you in the
Harvest Moon of your desires.

Rising above the elements of an earthly life,
Dancing with the echoes of her deepest beauty.
Woman delights in a journey of self-awareness
With her soul and heart.
Like the dolphin and sea who live as one,
In harmony woman and soul embrace
Their harmony as a majestic
Journey through thought and breath.

Woman will rise from troubled waters
Riding on the back of triumph.
Her garment is weaved in the victory
Of desire and her cloak is anointed in the
Knowledge of the angels.
Woman will journey this day undaunted by
The chatters of her adversaries as she is lifted
By that which paints the stars.
And is the consciousness of all that she loves.

When a woman looks into the water well of her life,
It is her soul that calls to quench the thirst for love
And wisdom that awaits her between the worlds.

When a woman silently suffers the clanging chains
Of her past and takes the role of servant
To the yowling echoes of her pain?
Who then will call the angels to weep for her?
What ghosts laugh in the night and whisper lies of
Self-blame and hatred to her?
For it is a Godless creature that taunts the mind
Of the confused and weakened lives of the woman
Who clings to the edge of a cliff as she seeks to
Climb the higher path of self-love and truth.
Yet she will hear the song of the rain.
The laughter of the storm, and the calling
Of the light as she trudges the journey
Of happy destiny.
And she will be wrapped in a blanket of love
Weaved by the Goddess of the heavens,
For she is woman and is created in the
Divine Consciousness of Love.

Woman will sing with the voice of her ancestors.
As her song will inter-twine the sun rays,
Like two loops dancing in the sky as one.
Her voice of love and oneness flows
With the light of infinity.

When a young girl dances in the rain
The rain dances back with her.
And all women are the dance of a young girl
When love paints the colors of their heart.

*Woman rides a spiritual wave of enlightenment
This new dawn.
Like a leaf that frees itself from the bondage of a
Tree and rides the wind.
She has washed her thoughts in the flowing
Light of oneness.
Like the rocks in the bed of a river
As the water flows over them.
Woman follows her path, as if it were music
Coming from a finely tuned instrument.*

The Divine Feminine Consciousness
Awakens a Woman.
As the morning dawn washes the sleep
From her eyes.
The angel of the sun will embrace
Her awakened breath.
And the angel of the air will merge
With her life forces.
For woman knows she is her highest truth
As she journeys through this day.

In a woman's awakening of self-realization
She will hold the power of her world
Between the worlds
In the consciousness of her love and oneness
Through soul and eternity.

Woman is the manifestation
Of the Divine Feminine Consciousness.
Her journey is a prayer of love and peace,
Her thoughts are like a soft breeze.
Like still waters reflecting the stars and the moon,
Her heart reflects the Kingdom of Love.

Her Soul is the breath of God
That the angels breathe, for they have merged
Into the consciousness of all that is.
As woman and soul are one, she will bathe
In the light and dance upon the earth
Her consciousness of love is the awakened path.

*As a woman listens to the oneness of her universe
She will touch the hearts of the angels around her.
She will dance with the consciousness of all
Creation as though it was the only thought
One could have.
And the flowers will flourish in the garden
Of her life with the colors of her heart.
For she carries the message of love
In every breath she takes.*

As a Woman thinks and believes she will create
In the reflection that surrounds her.
She will walk amongst the angels as they clear the
Path of her beliefs…
Just as a flower will grow in the garden of heaven,
It is one with the universe.
For the flower knows the gardener will till the
Ground and clear away the weeds…

As the voice on the edge of the forest calls the wolf
"come, come and be one with me."
The voice in between the worlds calls to Woman
And says … "come, come to me and we will unite in
The oneness of the sisterhood of both worlds.
And we will bring forth the Kingdom of Peace and
Love to rein over all the people."

Each star has a name by which it is called.
Every flower wears the colors from which it is born.
Wild beasts of the forest fall in love
With one another.
Just as all women have a dream laced in gold
That they treasure......

I say young girl, I'm talking to you!
Live a life of compassion, accept all
For whom they are.
Love everyone, and most of all love yourself.
Set boundaries to live by and use them.
Cast the weeds from your garden of life
And cultivate the company you keep.
As you shall grow to live by the colors of your heart,
And then you will dance with true love.

In Spirit there is a song, one heard by all
In creation who listen.
It moves through all life forces as though it were
pulling us closer to the Oneness of your live.
The giant beasts and woman will dance with each
other for they know the song so well.

In the beginning the Divine Feminine
Consciousness gave birth to woman.
She stood upon the earth in the light and love
That surrounded her while the angels sang a
Glorious song of her arrival.
And she sang back a poem, a prayer, to be heard
By all births that were to follow.
She sang the song of oneness into eternity.

*In the Divine Consciousness of Love we hear the
Whispers of a woman's prayer.
Her Spirit dances upon the wind as her essence is
The sweet fragrance of the garden.
We will see her joy, her laughter and her harmony
In the balance of nature.
And in the reflection of the still waters, her beauty
Will ascend above all earthly matters.*

In the forest woman will build her altar
From the elements that surround her
As she raises her chalice to heaven.
She will sip from her cup with the angels
As though it were the Holy Grail
Filled with the creative loving energy of all life.
And she will quench her thirst for wisdom and truth
As she journeys down a path of self-realization.

Inspired by the roar of the oceans,
Guided only by the spirit of the wind.
Woman will race on the whispers of her knowledge
That her love for freedom and spirit are one with
Her world, as her world is one with the universe.

Butterfly Woman will touch the heart
Of the music in the morning dawn.
As the Joy of all flowers is in the dance
She brings to the garden of life.
So beautiful to look upon is the gift
Of a woman who has freed herself from
The cocoon as her journey is the music
Of a new day.

The Awakened Woman delights in her path
Of self-realization.
Like a meadow of flowers welcomes the rain
To help them grow.
Woman welcomes the Consciousness of Love
As her food for Truth.
Her path to Love and Truth is the same path
As the stars are to the heavens.

*There will be no separation between the
Woman and the music.
For they are one in the experience of life.
Like the Angels that descend from the
Kingdom of Heaven and takes the spirit
Of the wolf, they are one in the dance.
Woman stands on the edge of her forest
As the music plays and the Angels descend,
For she is one with the wolf.*

Where is the story of the awakened
Woman recorded?
But in the poetry of the stars.
Like the whispering wind in the night,
Or in the song of the rising sun.
Her awakened birth created in the
Consciousness of love,
And weaved into the blanket of her life.
As if it were poems written upon the flowing river
Told to all who came to quench their thirst.
And sung deep in the forest night, like a lullaby
That cradles the creatures as they sleep.
Awakened is the woman who listens to the wisdom
Of her soul that communes with all life
And walks a path designed by the stars.

What a Woman seeks on her journey,
She has already embraced and drank tea with,
In her heart.
She has stood upon the mountain and whispered
Her poems to the stars and she has stood before
The ocean and listened to the wisdom of the whales.
Woman has traveled across the desert and
Drank from the well of knowledge.
For she will stand between the worlds in the
Consciousness of her universe as she journeys
With truth and soul.

Wild is the woman who rides on the wind
Of her thoughts for a better life.
Chased by a river of music, washed by a
Song of love, she shines in the light.
Eagles will soar in the skies, as wolfs will
Howl at the moon for woman's journey.
For she is the gypsy upon the mountain top
In the story she will tell.

Woman dresses herself in a garment of light as
She steps into the sacred circle of her life.
Her arms sway as feet move to the music
Of the night, ancient drums beat in her heart.
She will call upon the elements of her mother,
And draw down the stars into her circle.
The Ancestors hear her calling, the angels dance
around her circle, she is the moon woman.

Woman hears the morning angel singing as she
Awakens to the path of her golden dawn.
She dresses herself with the enlightened music that
Echoes in her thoughts of a new day.
As she touches the heart of her reflection in the
Mirror, oneness of love touches her back.
Woman greets her day accompanied with the
Self-realization, that she is light and soul choosing
To experience life.

Woman is a Divine Soul experiencing life's journey.
Like the butterfly that touches flowers sipping
Nectar with joy and pleasure.
She dances across the sky embracing each moment
In the sun light as she glitters with laughter of love
For her life.

Woman is the Divine Feminine Consciousness
Of our universe.
She is the face that looks upon us from the Stars
In the heavens.
The Garden of Life is cultivated in the heart
Of every woman.
For she is the voice in the soul on a journey
Into the light and love of eternity.

Woman is the morning glory of the dawn,
She is the rising sun.
An awakened light shining upon the earth
Woman walks.
Her light bends around her thoughts,
Like a flower following the sun.
As her Oneness of being embraces truth,
She follows her light.

Woman is the voice of history, she is the memory
Of the stars.
Woman is the design in a butterfly's wing,
The poem of the angels.
She is the silence in the forest and the song
Of the wind.
Her essences is like the oil that anoints the rain
As it falls upon the
Flowers and gives rise to the fragrance of peace
And love around the world.

*Moon Woman and the Sister of Eternal Life dance
In the Divine Consciousness of Oneness.
They know their power is in all women of the world,
In their song, in their breath, and in their heart.
For as each Woman stands in the light of the Moon,
The heavens hear their words and the eternal light
Shines down upon them all.*

*Woman stands on the clouds and touches the rain
With blessing as it falls upon the earth.
She will touch the heart of the rainbow and raise
Her hand to the rays of the sun sending her love to
All to be touched by the light.
Dancing on the wind like an eagle in the sky with a
Song of peace and kindness she will send
Her love around the world.
As all the people will hear her song and heal.*

Woman tells the world "Love is not blind.
Love will only see your highest good,
Your purest truth and your greatest beauty"!
Woman tells the world
"Only when you see less than that, does love
become blind."

*Woman will hear the whispers of her song coming
from the mountain tops, as she dances in the dream
Time of her dawn.
She will awaken to angels gathering around her
To bathe her with love and dress her in a garment
Of sun light and flowers for they know she is
On a path of new beginnings.*

Woman will hold her thoughts of the world
In her hands as though it were the
Precious breath of a child.
She will pull it close to her heart as she dances
In the light of all life. For she wears the kingdom
Of her heaven as she journeys down a path
Of love and compassion to heal
The world around her.

Woman, raise your head to the rising sun
Of the east and hold your ear the whispers
Of the dawn.
The song you hear is the echo of your
Highest calling from the
Divine Feminine Consciousness of all life.
Hold your hands to the sky and dance in rhythm
With the air around you and the ground
You walk upon.
As your path is one with the world and the world
Is one with you.

*Woman, open the window of your heart and breathe
In the light of love.
Recite the poems of the angels recorded by your
Soul and breathe.
Open the door to our mind and slide down a
Rainbow of joy and laughter, into a pool of loving
Consciousness as you bathe yourselves in the warm,
Gentle love of your highest truth.*

Woman will dance upon the rainbows
In all her glory.
She will shout out to the world from
The mountain tops.
Woman knows her oneness, her truth,
Her Path, as the eagle soars above the clouds
Her spirit rides the wind of love.

Woman is like the angel of the garden, cultivated by
The consciousness of oneness.
For blessed is the fruit of her life as the fragrance
Of her words sing to all people of the world.
It is in her garden of wisdom that others will come
To harvest her knowledge of peace and compassion
On their journey through life.
Her garden of love is ever growing as we seek this
Angel of the garden we call woman.

55

Woman chants her mantras to the dawn
For the rising sun calls her.
She will breathe in the angel of the sun
To purify her thoughts, her breath, her words.
Like the wild stallion that dances across the desert
In freedom of spirit.
Woman will dance this day in her freedom
Of spirit and life.

As Woman ends her day and lays her head to rest,
She prepares for a journey between the worlds.
She will meet with her equal in Angels, and soar
Through the heavens of light.
It is in this place woman dances with laughter
And joy in the heart of all creation.
In her dream time woman quenches her thirst
For truth and wisdom on her path into infinity.

Woman awakens to the song of the
Angel of the sun.
She will meditate upon her breath and call
In the angel of the air.
Loving herself and all life she rides on the wings
Of the angel of light.
Dressed with the angel of love she greets
Her day of new beginnings.

What can make the stars sing upon the night,
But a woman who can unfold her thoughts
Of love and light.
Who can pull a rainbow from the sky and lay
A path to dance upon, but a woman who touches
Her heart and sings of a glorious journey.

Is it not in the fragrance of a rose that tells the story
Of the majestic woman and Sprit that ride the wind
And sails the sea of love.
Is it not the angels of heaven that chase
Her laughter and song.
Yet it is the wild creatures of the forest
That walk with her.
And the eagles who soar the sky around her.
For she is not a dream but a reality
Awakened in a new dawn.

Woman delights in the nectar of her life.
Her heart is like a river flowing in harmony with all
That it touches.
Like an angel planting flowers beneath the sun,
Woman dances with each new dawn as if she was in
A garden of love and light.

Above the galaxy she came from,
She looks to the light,
Touching this light with her mind,
She feels the connection.
The warm and soothing voice that follows
Tells her: welcome our child we love you so much,
We are here for you.

In her meditation she has no questions,
She seeks no answers.
She awaits truth through the voice of her soul
And finds the light in her heart.
As all darkness dissipates away,
She rises in the light.
Now she sees the truth,
That her consciousness of oneness
With her world is the path.

Touch the silence of your mind.
Let us raise our consciousness above all doubts
And follow our soul as we walk through
The heaven of our life.
Here on earth let us live this day in peace
And harmony with ourselves and all who's
Path we cross.
This is the voice of our Soul who walks
Amongst the Gods.

In the sanctuary of your mind touch the heart
Of silence, listens only to the presence of love.
This place of beauty heals you.
Let the warm arms of silence wrap around you,
As you ascend to the heavens of your consciousness
And touch the breath of all creation.

Journey the path of your true beauty
And see the truth of who you really are.
Open the windows of your mind and breathe
In the fresh scent of love that awaits you.
Touch the heart of joy, and hold hands
With your angels as they dance you.
Greet each thought you have with kindness
And compassion and embrace
The all loving woman you are.
You are so beautiful.

Let a woman meditate on love,
Compassion and kindness.
Let her listen to her soul as she journeys
In to the silence.
The light will touch her and her world
Will be one of peace.

Breathe with the angel of the air.
This angel that is in all life, which spreads the sweet
Smell of the mysteries of our garden.
Let us breathe this messenger of the most high that
Touches every cell of our being.
As she brings the secrets of the wind
In your meditation.
She is the angel that connects us to the oneness as
We dance upon our earthly mother.

68

Clear your mind and call upon the angel of water
To open the gate of heaven and rain down upon
Your thoughts and cleanse you of your impurities.
Oh messenger of the highest, wash our thoughts
In your song of love, fill our now empty vase
With thoughts of compassion and kindness
That we may dance together with all the angels
And touch each other's lives with gentleness.

Open the gates of your consciousness and inter
The kingdom of love and compassion.
We shall dance in the heart of our God
As we walk through meadows
Of beautiful butterflies and flowers.
We will hear the songs of the angels
As we bathe our thoughts in the light of glory
And carry this message to everyone we meet.
For we have awakened
To the consciousness of oneness.

As you journey inward you find
The most beautiful creation of all.
A gentle, loving, colorful creation
That has journeyed the whole while.
Hold this creation in the highest of thoughts,
The highest of words and touch this gift with your
Heart of delight and laughter and love.
As you meditate see the golden light
And greet this gift within you,
Listen to what they say
There will be no greater words of love.

As woman quietly walked through the forest
She heard a tree whisper to her "let us dance."
As she look upward in the forest trees and saw
A mist, that spelled out the word "MAGIC"
She looked up even higher and saw the branches
Swaying, but there was no wind.
Woman was compelled to dance, so she did.
These are the thoughts of a woman as she sits
On a rock in the hot sun freeing her mind.

Embrace the consciousness of oneness,
Let your spirit dance,
Be the vibration of love that you are.
Listen to the song of your heart that beats to the
Rhythm of your soul.
Hear the Spirit of your creation calling you,
And rejoice in the connection of your awakening.

Woman will plow the fields of her mind.
She will choose only the finest thoughts to plant.
She will cultivate her garden and cast
The ugly weeds of thought out by their roots.
And when she harvests the crops, woman will
rejoice in joy as she reaps what she has sown.

Meditate on the angel of the sun and feel
Her kisses and warmth upon your body.
Call on the angel of the water
And wash all doubt in your life away,
Breathe the angel of the air and fill your body
With the spirit of love, call on the angel
Of mother earth as you feel the joy of
Oneness in your life.

When a woman meditates and she touches the heart
Of her kingdom of heaven, like liquid pouring out
Of a glass, it fills her with knowledge,
Wisdom and love.
She will know the full cycle of life
When she looks at a single blade of grass.
She will understand love of all life
And rejoice in the giving breath.
So filled by the light will be her path
As she touches the heart in her kingdom of heaven.

Meditate upon the angel of the light and welcome
Her into the temple of your body.
Open the windows and all the doors to your temple
That she may bring in her light and warmth
And cast all darkness out, for she is a messenger
Of truth and healing that dances with your soul.
And gives rise to your spirit of joy.
This angel of the light in all her beauty and glory
comes from the most high.

In the beauty of her light, she has but one thought.
In her soul she hears but one voice, she knows only
One thing with all certainty that she is
Her highest good, created by the source
Of all creation, focusing on the light and love
She does her work.

When a woman meditates she will touch the
Consciousness of her creation.
She will walk through the halls of her mind
Pouring bottles of liquid golden light
Over her thoughts as she clears her head.
Woman stands in the silence of the universe
With the creative source of love
As the light paints the colors of her heart.

Woman will meditate in a fashion that opens her
Mind to the silence of her thoughts.
Where her breath is one with her universe
And only one heart beats for all life.
It is there she will dance with the voice of her heart,
As she listens to the song of wisdom
And enlightenment, a sanctuary designed by her
For a time to heal and grow.

Hear the song of your birth,
The voice of your soul
Sings with such beauty.
In the meadows of your mind
Dance freely to this song,
Feeling the rhythm of the universe
Moving through you.
As you dance with your angels
And listen to the song
Of this beautiful creation.

In her mind she will sit upon a mountain of love.
She will breathe in the air of kindness
And exhale compassion for all people of the world.
Woman will meditate as though she was an empty
Vase surrounded by the consciousness
Of her creative loving energy filling her thirst
With truth and wisdom.

Climb the stairs to the door of your consciousness.
Open the ears of your mind and listen
To the glorious song of love.
You will enter the light of the loving creative energy
This source of all life and see the reflection
Of whom you really are.
Hold your angel's hand, enter with them, that you
May touch the oneness of your eternity.

In the Kingdom of your Heart, listen to the voice
Of your Creator speak through your soul.
Feel the breath of love touch your life as you walk
The path of peace and balance for all creation.
Life is a chosen experience that continues
To bring you closer to the highest truth.
That life is the Consciousness of Love within you.

In a woman's meditation she will breathe in the love
Of her God and see the golden light of that love
Surround her every thought.
Listen to the light as it awakens you to the path
Of self-realization, compassion, and kindness.
She will touch the heart of all creation in this
Oneness of life as she breathes.

Free your mind of thoughts that weigh you down,
That burden you with doubt and fear.
Turn your focus to your breath, to the beat
Of your heart, and then,
Just think about the breath of the wind
In your face and how lite that feels.

Woman will touch the heart of her thoughts and
Allow her mind to open up to the voice of her soul.
As she will seek a path of understanding
And wisdom for all creation.

Take the time to listen to the wind in the trees
And follow the heart of your path.
See the colors of your consciousness
In the silence of your mind,
As you hear the sparrows sing of love
And joy in their hearts.
Touch the still waters of your mind
And bathe in the peace that it brings to you.

The woman who sits in quiet contemplation of her
Heart and soul is in good company.
Make your thoughts of a more gentle love.
Close your eyes and draw in the beauty of your
World as you welcome all life around you.
Listen to the oneness of your breath entering your
Heart, filling you with joy
For life and love.

The Book of Eve

You are the first thought, the first breath,
The first Soul in the manifestation of
Our creation called Woman.
And our Creator will dress you
In flesh and bone through the womb
Of our mother earth.
You are created through all matter and thought,
And created autonomously with no preconception
Of love or oneness. All things you touch and see
Hold the breath of our Creator within them.
Your breath is their breath as you stand
Independently attuned to all things around you.
You are whole and complete in the creation
Of all life around you.
As the air feeds fire, the water will quench the thirst
Of all plants and creatures of the mother earth.
And each has a language of which you understand
For there is no separation in our being.
Only the art of oneness.

Our oneness of being is in the consciousness
From above the stars, above the galaxies and above
The Kingdom of Heaven.
For our soul is birthed by the Supreme Divine
Feminine energy of light which only infinity
Has touched. It is here in a timeless and space less
existence that love flows through the consciousness
of our creator.
That which we are told is eternity was birthed from
Above and comes from our Father whose
Consciousness created all matter of what we call the
Kingdom of Heaven and all that descends from it.
It is here the heart learned to beat, as the soul was
Conceived in the womb of our Mother of Infinity.
The good news I bring to you is recorded upon the
Stars through the consciousness of love and weaved
Into each soul born, prior to its incarnation here
Upon our mother earth.
It is from this love of oneness for all life we walk in
The garden, as the garden is in all things.
There is no place outside the garden, for the garden
Is a path of the heart.
All forms of life reside in the garden; all elements
Upon our Mother are in harmony with the garden.
In the garden we bathe our body and thoughts.
In the garden we hear the music and dance with the
Wind.
In the garden we choose our course and set sail
For a thousand journeys.
Each journey bringing us closer to that timeless
And space less existence of love.
Where once again we will touch the face of Infinity.

We are created in a world where all life is equal,
Where no life is greater than another.
From the smallest life form, to the giant creatures
That walk the land, our light force is the same.
As a single blade of grass is created in the same
Light the mighty oak tree is created in.
The water we drink and wash our face in,
Is equal to the sun that kisses our skin.
The fire we dance around is equal to the wood it
Burns and the drum we carry is equal to the eagle
That soars above the mountain tops.
For true harmony has no boundaries or limitations
It only knows oneness.
And it is the image of oneness that all things are
Created in, and that oneness
Is the Light of Love the Divine Feminine
Consciousness, the face of Infinity in all things.
As you are the first thought, the first breath,
The first Soul in the manifestation of our creation
Called woman, and we walk upon our mother earth
In multitudes.
Our journey is one, yet there will be as many paths
Along this journey as there are stars above.
Hold one hand up to the light and the other upon
Our heart, as it is the heart that communes with the
Light and in our stillness we listen to them talk.
The Journey is not a quest for answers, but is a
Desire to experience life.
We learn, the path that is chosen, is created by
Desire.
We create these experiences in union with the light
For our desires.

Just as the fire desires to burn,
It is our desire to warm our bodies and
Light up the night.
Fire is the journey the path is one of warmth
And light.
Let your path cross with the multitudes there
Will be more warmth and light.

For our journey is with all creation and
All creations shall journey.
All souls are birthed from the
Divine Feminine Consciousness into
The Kingdom of Heaven as souls
 Then descended to this path, and dressed by
Our mother earth in the garden.
As the Kingdom is reined by the
Consciousness of God the breath of life.
The Soul is the child of that marriage.
So as it is recorded upon the stars and weaved into
Our soul we will know the Spiritual Trinity as:
The Divine Feminine Consciousness,
The Consciousness of our father God and the Soul.
Let us walk our path in the name of the Mother,
The Father, and the Soul ….
On this path in this garden with the multitudes
There is amongst us that whish is
Born, which travels from Kingdom to mother earth
Yet is not dressed in the garden but dressed in the
Kingdom, and we shall call them angels.
They are like the air and move like the wind,
dressed in a prism of colors, with a voice like the
whispers of a smooth flowing river.
Sent as a guardian, a messenger, a healing ever
Present love of light this born soul exists with us
And all life around us, these souls we call angels.
For it is written upon the stars "even a single flower
Has an angel to watch over it."
As this is the good news I bring, so it shall be.
And we shall gather around the table to bring
Nourishment to our flesh and bones.

Let us gather around the table as we cross paths
And join each other in love and light.
Let us gather around the table and rejoice
In the glory of our being.
And we shall prepare a meal from
The garden as it is recorded upon the stars
And weaved into our soul.
As all life is in harmony, it is also in agreement
That upon our mother earth life will feed life.
Our mother earth feeds all life and all life
Shall feed each other.
The Desire of what will nourish one life will be
Autonomous to the next as the Consciousness of
God has filled the garden to meet all desires of
Texture, flavor, and nourishment.
It is in preparation and before we gather at the table
That which we touch carries our energy and
Thoughts.
Make this the time to raise your hand to the face of
Infinity and place your other hand upon your heart.
This is the time to cleans your thoughts and prepare
With a glorious song to the Most High.
To prepare a meal with love strengthens the path of
Another on their journey as well as your own.
At the time that the last bite has been eaten and all
Have had their fill, it is then you should embrace
Each other and give words to the Most High what
Has come from the garden and bless each other's
Path with harmony, safe travels and joyous
Experiences till the next time you meet.

Do all things in the garden, for the garden is a
Path of the heart.
Always embrace each other in the garden,
Bless each other in the garden.
Speak only from the garden.
Make your prayers in the garden.
Prepare your food in the garden.
Bathe yourself and others in the garden
Dress yourself and others in the garden.
Create all music in the garden,
As you sing in the garden.
For your dawn will always rise in the garden,
And that is where your sun will set.
We are a multitude of souls in the garden
Each on a path through the journey into Infinity.
We will cross many paths on this journey, as some
Paths will look like yours, you must first listen to
Their prayers to see where in the garden they grow.
As many flowers will look the same the fragrance
They offer may not wear so will on you.
In the garden all life is in harmony, each will
Complement the garden with their unique
Differences.
Our relationship with all life is recorded upon the
Stars and woven into our soul as each soul carries
These records they draw from their star.
Do not mistake another's star for yours, and do not
try to make your star belong to another.
But let the stars dance beneath the heavens in
Harmony before your eyes, and dance with the
Music they bring.

Write your good news upon a leaf and then hold the
Leaf to the wind and allow the wind to carry the
Good news throughout the garden.
And if you find a stick on your path and you see a
Beautiful flute in that stick, carve the flute and play
The music of your star. Or write a prayer upon the
Stick and leave it lay for other's to find.
But let no other tells you what to write upon your
Leaf or tell you how to carve your flute.

To write, to play music, to draw art upon a rock and
To dance are all expressions
Of one's soul feeding the flesh and the will of our
Being, as it is our soul that nourishes our body in
Soul.
For it is our soul that is birthed from the
Mother of Infinity.
And she is all things above all things created.
As she is pure the soul is pure.
As she is untainted the soul is untainted.
As she is not fettered the soul is not fettered.
As she does not hunger the soul does not hunger.
For the oneness of soul is pure and created without
Sin through the Mother of Infinity and the Father
Of Heaven into the flesh and all other life form
Upon our mother earth.
As a tree is not born with sin, no child is born of sin.
As our soul is one with the soul of wild horses we
Are born without sin.
We are born not with a hungry soul as no light can
Hunger for more light.
Our Soul too lacks nothing in its existence.
It is the desire of our path that hungers, as it is the
Path of a tree to hunger for sun and rain.
For we are the voice; the first thought, the first
Breath, the first soul in the manifestation of our
creation called woman.
And this is my leaf, my flute, and my dance
Recorded upon my star and written across my heart.
All in the name of the Mother, the Father
And the Soul.
We are a multitude in the garden, our journey is
Oneness, our path is desire and we are all created

Individually, crossing paths, sharing leaves and at
Times dancing together.
As the rain will share its soul with the flowers of the
Meadow, as the flowers will share their nectar with
The butterfly.
As the rain does not give up its path to the meadow,
The flower does not give up its path to the butterfly.
The partnership is one of harmony and union.
Let it be the same for you in your partnerships and
Let us not give up our path for another, but share
Our nectar in harmony and union.

It is in our relations with all creation that we will
Dance with the reflections of who we are.
It is in our partnerships with one another that we
Will write our songs to the Most High.
As all life has been created in the image of the
Consciousness of God.
For even a single blade of grass is created in the
Image of the Most High and journeys a path in the
Garden.
So it is all life upon our mother earth will carry the
Breath of the Consciousness of God who reigns in
The Kingdom of Heaven and all that descends from
The Heaven.
As our feet touch the grass, as our hand holds the
Flower, as we wash our bodies beneath the
Waterfalls and we lay upon the cliffs to be kissed by
The sun we will feel the Consciousness of God
Touching our lives.
Let us hold each other in this consciousness as we
Cross the paths of our desires.
We are on a journey of oneness with all things, as
This is written on the leaves that ride on the soul of
The wind.
And it will be in the soul of the fire, the flames of
Desire, we will dance with each other in the music
We create to echo our love for one another.
And in the stillness of our garden let us paint our
Prayers of communion upon the soul of water as
We bathe our children of oneness and hold them to
The light.

As it will be, when we touch the heart of our
Mother Earth so shall we touch that, which has
been created in the image of God.
For I am the voice!
And these are my words I have written on the leaves
That ride the wind, and dance in the fire.
They are the words I paint upon the waters.
The words that are echoed back to woman as
She touches the heart of mother earth.
Let us raise our hand to the face of Infinity, and
Place our other hand upon our hearts in the name
of The Mother, the Father, and the Soul .....

As we awaken to the soul of the morning dawn
We are greeted by the sun and the music of his rays
Touch our cheeks with love and joy.
For the soul of the sun knows our journey is one.
As I have sailed the Milky Way upon the wings of
The angels from the Kingdom of Heaven in my
dreams.
Where I have entered other worlds with gardens of
Of love and joy for all who journeyed.
With rivers that play music as they flow and
Mountains that whisper mantras that fed the
Bodies of those who climb them.
It is there I also see the multitudes that travel the
Paths of oneness.
And our reflections greet each other in the face of
The Divine Feminine Consciousness,
Of our Mother of Infinity.
For it is there we awaken in the glorious love of that
Which births all souls into the Consciousness of
God and the eternity of all life.
And as we have awakened to the glorious love on
this path, we have awakened to the path of the
butterfly and its oneness with the sky.
Let us see, that the glorious flight of the butterfly is
Equal to the glorious flight of the eagle in our
Garden.
For it is truly our reflection we look upon, and our
Oneness with all life that we see.
Let us play our flutes and dance with the butterfly
And the eagle, let us beat our drums in harmony
With the heartbeat of the great oak tree.

Let us run with the leopard, roar with the lion, and
Walk with the camel through the soul of the desert.
As the wind touches our face and combs our hair.
Let the journey of oneness direct your path as this
Is the true Consciousness of God and the path
Through eternity.
As it will be the soul of eternity that guides you to
The face of Infinity.
For this is the good news I write
Upon the leaves in the wind.

Our relationship with the Consciousness of God,
Our Father who reigns over the
Kingdom of Heaven and all that descends from the
Kingdom is and always will be a direct
Consciousness upon our hearts.
As is our relationship with that which is above the
Kingdom of Heaven, that which birthed all souls,
And she is our Mother of Infinity,
The Mother of all things that are and are not. The
Mother of all worlds, all plains, all gardens and all
Journeys, she is the face of Infinity.
And we are the flesh of this Consciousness as are
All things that we can see and touch and all things
We cannot see and touch.
Let us Love this Consciousness with all our heart,
In all our thoughts, in all that we believe and do.
For are time to worship will not differ from our
Paths and the way you worship must come from
Your heart.
Let the Consciousness of Love the voice of your
Soul teach you how to worship, and if what you do
Flows as smoothly with you as the waters flow with
The river and you feel your connection to the
Mother and the Father rise with joy in that
Relationship, like the flames rise with a good fire
Then this is truly a path with heart.
As you will know, the waters flows with the river
Headed down the mountain and through the
valleys, not up the mountain.
And a fire's flame will not rise without dry wood.
So will it be as you worship, what is in harmony
With your heart will flow and rise to the
Highest Truth.

For the Consciousness of God speaks clearly
To those who listen to their heart.
No one person's leaves will be the right leaves for
All, so share your written leaves of worship, but
Make them true for no one but yourself, and be wise
Not to judge another's worship for you know not
Their relationship with the Consciousness of God.
As the word of God is written upon the hearts of all
Living creatures in a way that they will understand
For themselves.
And let us worship in the garden, for the garden is
A path of the heart.

All that we are comes to us from in the garden.
As a butterfly will never lose its beautiful colors,
We shall never lose our gifts from the garden.
Let us sow these gifts in our songs, and write them
Upon our leaves. Let us cultivate our thoughts like
The farmer who cultivates their crops and harvest
Golden wheat to make their bread to
Feed their families.
For it is what we think that we plant.
Let us treasure these gifts we are, but hoard
Them not.
Be like a rose that blooms and shares its scent,
As the rose bud that does not open will wither,
Dry up, and die.
Be not that rose bud that does not open on your
Path.
See your reflection in all things; embrace all paths
You cross with love and kindness.
Like our sister eagle embraces the wind as she
Spreads her wings to fly,
Higher she will go, her path is one of freedom.
Dress your feet with the Kingdom of Heaven, your
Words with the Consciousness of God,
Wear the garment of the angels and bless all life
Through the Mother of Infinity.
With this, you shall weave a life of the oneness of
Love and abundance for all.
And do these things in the name of our Mother, our
Father and Soul.
For you are the first thought, the first breath, the
First creation called woman
And we are in the multitudes.

To you I say; what of our brothers, our fathers,
Our husbands and our sons?
They too are Souls birthed from the Mother of
Infinity into the Consciousness of
God and descend from the Kingdom of Heaven
Upon our mother earth.
What of our relationships with them do we hold?
But that of your equal in the garden.
Let us live in the rapture of our delight, let us share
our gifts and our abundance of love with passion,
But suffer not these paths we cross, and lose
Ourselves in despair or submit to that which is not
In our garden.
Lose not your gifts nor forfeit the beauty of your life
To walk with another.
As it is with the eagle that flies across the glorious
Sky beneath the sun they will not fly so close to the
Sun as to burn their wings and fall, but fly in union
With the elements that surround them.
For your oneness and purpose is not in the life of
Another, but is with all life.
Be wise about your desires and forgiving with your
Decisions.
Remember it is the heart that hears the voice of the
Soul, follow the path of your heart and suffer not
That which comes to you.
Be clear that the soul is birthed without a gender,
As love has no gender but only affection and desire
For union and to experience eternity.
As the Kingdom of Heaven is pure love we descend
In pure love, we are born unto this life without sin
As we have come from the heavens.

*Our Heavenly Father creates all things with love so
Shall all things return to the Kingdom of Heaven.
Wait not for another's path to be judged for it
Will not happen.
Each day raise one hand to the light, the mother of
Infinity and place your other hand over your heart,
As you listen to the voice of your soul, and you too
Will know all these things I say are true.*

Let us touch the breath of our children with
Our hearts.
Let us hold them as if they were the song of our
Breath and love, for they truly are.
As it is the Eve in every woman that will birth the
Masters, the gurus, the sages, and each prophet and
Messiah that walks through the garden and crosses
Paths with all who seek truth and the journey
Into eternity.
Let each woman raise her children as though she
Were the ocean and they were the sand on a beach,
As she washes over them with her knowledge of
Compassion and kindness for all creation.
Let her bathe them in the light of infinity that they
Know and commune with their soul.
Show them, they are the Consciousness of God as
They look into your eyes.
And their words will be that of the light as they
Learn.
For you women are the first breath, the first
Thought and the first creation they touch as they
Descend from the Kingdom of Heaven into our
Garden of life.
Teach them the glorious love of who they are,
Through the glorious love of who you are as they
Grow, and they will heal the weak, the sick and
The despaired who have blindly stepped out of
The garden.
Sing to them as the mountain sings to the valley, as
The rain sings to the earth, and as the stars sing to
The night.
And they will hear the melody of unity and oneness
For all creation in your song.

For then they will surly know you as Eve,
The soul of the Mother of Infinity and they too
Will lead the multitudes onto a joyous journey of
Peace and harmony with all life.

Echoes of Her Soul

*The Spiritual Woman follows the path of an
awakened heart.
Like a beautiful song follows the melody, woman
journeys into the Light.*
‚.•*¨"*•♫♪.♥

*The Woman who follows the path of light and love
knows the oneness of her creation and the journey
of her Soul.*
‚.•*¨"*•♫♪.♥

*When woman stands beneath the waters that falls
from the sky.
She knows it is the Kingdom of Heaven washing her
in the Oneness of Love.*
‚.•*¨"*•♫♪.♥

*A wise woman speaks softly on the path of Oneness,
for she knows the truth is but a whisper
from the light.*
‚.•*¨"*•♫♪.♥

*The woman, who quiets her mind before she sleeps,
will hear the songs of her God like lullabies to
dream by.*
‚.•*¨"*•♫♪.♥

The woman, who adheres to the journey of her heart as she sleeps, will ride upon the wings of an angel to a dream land above the stars created only for her.
.¸.●*¨¨*●♫♪.♥

Delighted in the awakening of a new dawn, Woman dresses her day with the colors of her heart.

.¸.●*¨¨*●♫♪.♥

The Woman who wraps herself in a blanket of light and love before she sleeps, will lay in the warmth of an Angels wings around her as she dreams.
.¸.●*¨¨*●♫♪.♥

Like the lotus sprout beneath the waters, Woman will transcend her thoughts towards the Light above, and grow to blossom in all her beauty.
.¸.●*¨¨*●♫♪.♥

Even when a woman closes her eyes and wanders through the darkness of her mind, she will still be standing in the light.
.¸.●*¨¨*●♫♪.♥

Each new day is like a work of art for the woman who creates herself a path of joy.
For she will paint her thoughts with a brush of pleasure and love for who she is.
.¸.●*¨¨*●♫♪.♥

*Her Soul has borrowed flesh and bone from her
mother earth, to walk amongst us. For she is more
than the eye and mind can conceive.
This Spirit of Light we call Woman.*
¸.•*¨'*•♫♪.♥

*A woman's love is the nectar of a flower that a man
seeks to dance on the palate of his desire.*
¸.•*¨'*•♫♪.♥

*When a Woman feels empowered,
She follows her higher calling.*
¸.•*¨'*•♫♪.♥

*Women who seek the company of the angels and a
good cup of tea, find pleasure in their
thoughts of life.*
¸.•*¨'*•♫♪.♥

*When a man loves a beautiful flower he will
instinctively not want to change even one petal on it.
Let him love his woman the same way.*
¸.•*¨'*•♫♪.♥

*Woman stands in the sun light listening to the
whispers of the wind.
As though it were her Angels singing a glorious
song of her journey.*
¸.•*¨'*•♫♪.♥

Woman knows her Oneness with life is in her Consciousness of the Universe and all creation. That is her Path.
.·•*"*•♫♪.♥

An enlightened woman will not seek to be understood, she just enjoys the company of likeminded people.
.·•*"*•♫♪.♥

In a woman's thoughts, she lays in a field of love as she listens to the angels sing.
.·•*"*•♫♪.♥

Like the wolf that runs through the forest feeling her freedom,
Woman dances with the thoughts of her wildness.
.·•*"*•♫♪.♥

The Awakened Woman teaches the Path of Oneness.
Her journey is based on truth.
.·•*"*•♫♪.♥

The woman who holds a single seed in her palm and sees the cycle of life, can dance in between the worlds and draw them together as one path.
.·•*"*•♫♪.♥

There is joy and peace found in the life of the woman who meditates.
¸.•*¨*•♫♪.♥

The Woman who sees life through the eyes of her heart will live without hate.
¸.•*¨*•♫♪.♥

The Woman who adheres to the song of her heart will not follow a path of self-destruction.
¸.•*¨*•♫♪.♥

Every rose dreams of growing up and becoming a woman someday...
¸.•*¨*•♫♪.♥

Woman knows everything is a poem, as she knows all movement is a verse.
¸.•*¨*•♫♪.♥

Woman will dance with rain like the thunder will dance with lighting.
When rain is seen Woman will be heard......
¸.•*¨*•♫♪.♥

She who seeks to dance in the Consciousness of her God will turn the winds with the palm of her hand and change the colors of sun rays into the colors of a rainbow.
¸.•*¨*•♫♪.♥

Woman begins her day in the sacred temple
of her heart.
In the stillness of her meditation she is the glorious
Light of Love
The Oneness of creation, the journey of her Soul.
.˛•*¨˙*•♫♪.♥

Like the lotus sprout beneath the waters,
Woman will transcend her thoughts towards
The light of love, and grow to blossom
in all her beauty.
.˛•*¨˙*•♫♪.♥

Each new day is like a work of art for the woman
who creates herself a path of joy.
As she will paint her thoughts with a brush of
pleasure and love for whom she is.
.˛•*¨˙*•♫♪.♥

Delighted in the awakening of a new dawn, Woman
dresses her day with the colors of her heart
.˛•*¨˙*•♫♪.♥

Woman and Angels are like the flowers and the sky.
Together they create a dance to the song
only they can hear.
.˛•*¨˙*•♫♪.♥

When a woman closes her eyes and visualizes the silence, she can see the color of the wind as it softly blows by.
.·•*¨*•♫♪.♥

Like the Sun above our heads,
When a Woman Awakens to her Truth,
She shines like a Star of pure Light.
.·•*¨*•♫♪.♥

Woman knows she is not the shell
that walks this life
But that it is the pearl inside her shell
that is her true being.
.·•*¨*•♫♪.♥

Woman knows that above and beyond all else,
She must be loyal to her truth.
Her path ascends to one of love and self-realization.
.·•*¨*•♫♪.♥

The Woman who seeks the kingdom of her heart,
finds the garden of roses without thorns.
.·•*¨*•♫♪.♥

www.ingramcontent.com/pod-product-compliance
Lightning Source LLC
Chambersburg PA
CBHW072006060426
42446CB00042B/2004